Sagebrush Steppe Vegetation Monitoring in Hagerman Fossil Beds National Monument

UPPER COLUMBIA
BASIN NETWORK

UCBN

2012 Annual Report

Natural Resource Data Series NPS/UCBN/NRDS—2012/402

Devin S. Stucki

National Park Service
Upper Columbia Basin Network Inventory and Monitoring Program
Craters of the Moon National Monument and Preserve
Arco, Idaho 83213

Thomas J. Rodhouse

National Park Service
Upper Columbia Basin Network Inventory and Monitoring Program
63095 Deschutes Market Road
Bend, Oregon 97701

October 2012

U.S. Department of the Interior
National Park Service
Natural Resource Stewardship and Science
Fort Collins, Colorado

The National Park Service, Natural Resource Stewardship and Science office in Fort Collins, Colorado, publishes a range of reports that address natural resource topics. These reports are of interest and applicability to a broad audience in the National Park Service and others in natural resource management, including scientists, conservation and environmental constituencies, and the public.

The Natural Resource Data Series is intended for the timely release of basic data sets and data summaries. Care has been taken to assure accuracy of raw data values, but a thorough analysis and interpretation of the data has not been completed. Consequently, the initial analyses of data in this report are provisional and subject to change.

All manuscripts in the series receive the appropriate level of peer review to ensure that the information is scientifically credible, technically accurate, appropriately written for the intended audience, and designed and published in a professional manner.

Data in this report were collected and analyzed using methods based on established, peer-reviewed protocols and were analyzed and interpreted within the guidelines of the protocols.

Views, statements, findings, conclusions, recommendations, and data in this report do not necessarily reflect views and policies of the National Park Service, U.S. Department of the Interior. Mention of trade names or commercial products does not constitute endorsement or recommendation for use by the U.S. Government.

This report is available from Upper Columbia Basin Network Inventory and Monitoring Program (http://science.nature.nps.gov/im/units/ucbn/) and the Natural Resource Publications Management website (http://www.nature.nps.gov/publications/nrpm/).

Please cite this publication as:

NPS 300/117423, October 2012

Contents

Figures

Tables

Tables (continued)

Executive Summary

As part of the Upper Columbia Basin Network sagebrush steppe vital signs monitoring program, a survey of sagebrush steppe ecological condition was conducted in late May and early June 2012 Hagerman Fossil Beds National Monument following methods outlined in the Upper Columbia Basin Network monitoring protocol (Yeo et al. 2009). The plot-based surveys occurred within 5 sampling frames that are positioned along the Oregon Trail, the tops of benches, and along the bottomland adjacent to the Snake River. Much of the uplands of the park are inaccessible, consisting of steep and highly unstable unvegetated escarpments. Cover of exposed soil and of principal native and non-native plants or genera were estimated in 301 1 m^2 quadrats randomly placed throughout the sampling frames. Sample plot locations were drawn using a spatially-balanced random sampling design, the Generalized Random Tessellation Stratified (GRTS) design, which ensures a good representative random sample with good dispersion within each sampling frame. The Monument was also surveyed in 2009, reported by Rodhouse (2010). The Long Butte Fire burned most of the vegetated uplands in HAFO in August 2010 and the 2012 survey provides the first opportunity to evaluate the effects of the fire on vegetation change in the Monument. We provide some preliminary comparisons between conditions encountered in 2009 before the fire and in 2012.

In general there was a shift toward increased annual grass-dominated vegetation. All frames in HAFO had very high frequency and cover estimates of cheatgrass in 2012, generally higher than what was recorded in 2009. Big sagebrush cover was very low compared to 2009 pre-fire levels. Greasewood (*Sarcobatus vermiculatus*), which resprouts after fire, had the highest cover and frequency of any of the shrubs in 2012, followed by green rabbitbrush (*Chrysothamnus viscidiflorus*). No bluebunch wheatgrass was encountered during monitoring and steppe bluegrass, a low-stature and very disturbance-resistant native perennial bunchgrass, had the highest frequency and cover estimates for all frames. Other perennial native grasses that were encountered in few plots include squirreltail (*Elymus elymoides*), indian ricegrass (*Achnatherum hymenoides*) and Great Basin wildrye (*Leymus cinereus*). Tumbling mustard had a higher frequency and percent cover than any other nonnative invasive forb, occurring in nearly 28% of all plots. This species also appears to have increased in abundance in most frames between 2009 and 2012. Noxious weeds were not encountered within plots though some infestations of rush skeletonweed (*Chondrilla juncea*) and Scotch thistle (*Onopordum acanthium*) were encountered while moving between sampling areas. These areas were documented and the locations given to park resource management during the field season.

Acknowledgments

Special thanks to JoAnn Blalack, HAFO resource chief, for providing logistical support to Devin during the field season.

Introduction

Prior to Euro-American settlement, sagebrush steppe ecosystems in the Upper Columbia Basin extended across the eastern half of Washington and Oregon, and across the northern Great Basin of southern Idaho. Currently much of that ecosystem has been lost to development or substantially degraded as a result of livestock grazing, fire, non-native invasive plants, and recreational use. The UCBN has identified the ecological condition of sagebrush steppe vegetation as a high priority vital sign and monitoring of its condition is central to its monitoring program (Garrett et al. 2007). A long-term monitoring program that provides for regular evaluation of the status of the health of sagebrush steppe communities, and for identification of trends of ecosystem condition over time within and among parks within the network was implemented in 2008 (Yeo et al. 2009). The foundation of the sagebrush steppe monitoring protocol is a view of ecosystem health sustained by natural succession or natural variability within communities of native plants. Divergence of sagebrush steppe communities from these natural states (e.g., invasion by non-native plants, increased fire frequencies, long-term trends of increasing cover of exposed soil, declines in cover of principal native plants) signifies a loss of health, and monitoring provides park managers with feedback necessary for developing effective adaptive management strategies. Simple monitoring objectives follow directly from this view:

• Determine the status (current condition) and trends (change in condition over time) in the composition and abundance (cover) of principal native plant species in UCBN sagebrush steppe communities.

• Determine the status and trends in composition and abundance (cover) of principal invasive plant species, including exotic annual grasses, in UCBN sagebrush steppe communities.

• Determine the status and trend in the amount of exposed soil (cover), a fundamental indicator of soil stability.

This report summarizes the data collected in 2012 for Hagerman Fossil Beds National Monument (HAFO), and discusses comparisons with data collected in 2009 (Rodhouse 2010) prior to the 2010 wildfire, the Long Butte Fire, that burned most of the sampling frame areas (Figure 1).

Methods

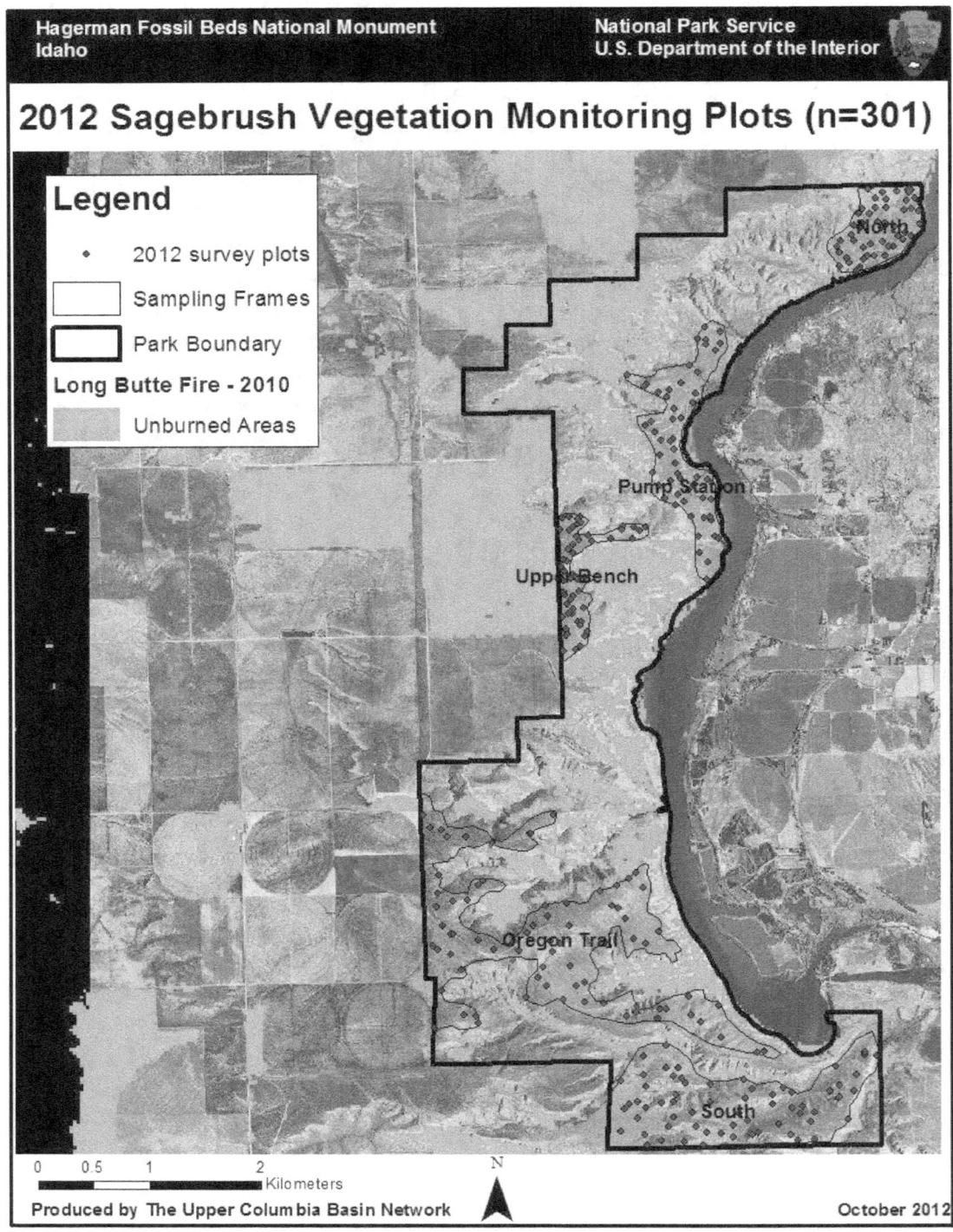

Figure 1. Hagerman Fossil Beds National Monument showing the 5 sampling frames surveyed in 2009 and 2012, with the 2012 plot locations. Areas unburned (estimated from Landsat imagery) are shown in green.

Sample sizes within each stratum were proportional to the area of each frame (Table 1). The total sample size in 2012 included one additional oversample plots from the GRTS list. Sampling procedures followed Yeo et al. (2009). Within each strata, 1-m² square plots were located using the generalized random tessellation stratified (GRTS) spatially-balanced sampling design (Stevens and Olsen 2004). The GRTS approach provides for randomly located plots and good spatial dispersion across each site. Within each 1-m² plot, we estimated cover of exposed bare ground and principal native plants and non-native invasive plants. Cover estimates were categorized into the following cover classes: 0, 1-5%, 5-25%, 25-50%, 50-75%, 75-95%, and 95-100% (Daubenmire 1959). Plant cover was defined as the natural spread of current year's growth outlined using a minimum convex polygon with small gaps included in the cover estimate. Exposed bare ground was defined as soil surface not overlain by plant cover, litter, and rock. Plant common names and their scientific names are listed in Appendix A.

Table 1. Sample sizes, by frame, for 2012 sagebrush steppe monitoring in HAFO. Details of frame development and target sample sizes are provided in Yeo et al. (2009).

Park	Sampling Frame	Sample Size
HAFO	North	50
HAFO	Oregon Trail	76
HAFO	Pump Station	55
HAFO	South	65
HAFO	Upper Bench	55
Total		301

Table 2. Daubenmire's cover classes used for visually estimating vegetation cover in 1 m² square quadrats.

Cover Class	Range	Midpoint
0	0%	0%
1	1-5%	2.50%
2	>5-25%	15%
3	>25-50%	37.50%
4	>50-75%	62.50%
5	>75-95%	85%
6	>95%	97.50%

Weather

Weather information was compiled from data obtained from the Hagerman 2 SW (103932) Weather Station outside of Hagerman, Idaho. This station is in close proximity (approximately 2 km) to the monument. Regionally, temperatures from winter through early summer in 2012 were very similar to 30 year average temperatures, though slightly higher, while precipitation had some larger than normal spikes early on and then fell by summer. Weather records are presented in Appendices C for those years going back to 2009 when we previously collected monitoring data in 2009.

Results and Discussion

The UCBN sagebrush steppe monitoring program completed a second season of monitoring in HAFO during May 21-25, 2012. Sample sizes ranged from 55 to 76 per sampling frame. HAFO was burned in 2010 by the Long Butte Fire which affected about 1215 ha (72% of monument) within monument boundaries. All frames sampled had been burned to some degree during the fire (Figure 1). A post burn reseeding project was developed but it is unclear at this point what management tactics have been employed. This second year of monitoring provides an interesting look at a landscape view of the sagebrush steppe vegetation within HAFO.

In general there was a shift toward increased bare ground between 2012 and 2009 (Appendix B). In 2012 more plots were encountered with bare ground estimates in high cover classes (>25%).

The proportion of plots containing native perennial grasses, native perennial forbs, and big sagebrush among the sampling frames that were sampled in 2012 can be found in Appendix B. Big sagebrush, which does not resprout after fire, was found in only the Oregon Trail, Pump Station, and South frames. These frames each had very low numbers of plots with big sagebrush cover. The Oregon Trail and South frames had only 1.3% and 1.5% proportions of plots with big sagebrush, and these plots had less than 5% big sagebrush cover. The Pump Station frame had 1.8% of plots with big sagebrush, with cover values between 5% and 25%. Greasewood (*Sarcobatus vermiculatus*), which does resprout after fire, had the highest cover and frequency of any of the shrubs, followed by green rabbit brush (*Chrysothamnus viscidiflorus*). Bluebunch wheatgrass (*Pseudoroegneria spicata*), a fundamental native perennial bunchgrass species included in potential natural vegetation descriptions for all parks under the UCBN sage monitoring protocol, was not encountered in any sample frame in HAFO in 2009 or 2012. Steppe bluegrass, a low-stature native perennial bunchgrass resilient to disturbance, was widespread in all 5 sampling frames and had the highest frequency and cover estimates for native grasses in all frames. Proportion of plots with >5% cover of steppe bluegrass ranged from 14% to 48%. The Upper Bench frame had the highest cover estimates for steppe bluegrass with almost 24% of plots having >25% cover for steppe bluegrass. Other perennial native grasses occurring less frequently and with less abundance when found included squirreltail (*Elymus elymoides*), followed by Indian ricegrass (*Achnatherum hymenoides*) and Basin wildrye (*Leymus cinereus*). Native forbs were found in 29% of plots in 4 panels. Strikingly, no native forbs were found in any plot in the North sampling frame. Most native vegetation was located on the tops of small ridges and swales or on mostly north facing inclines within drainages. Overall, native grass and forb presence was very low within the sampling frames in HAFO compared to monitoring data from 2009 (Rodhouse 2010, Appendix B).

No noxious weeds were encountered within plots, though some infestations of rush skeletonweed (*Chondrilla juncea*) and Scotch thistle (*Onopordum acanthium*) were encountered while travelling between plots. These infestations were documented and the locations were given to park resource management immediately. Figures in Appendix D show the proportion of plots in each frame estimated to contain cheatgrass (*Bromus tectorum*) in each of the 6 Daubenmire cover classes. Cheatgrass cover was ubiquitous and occurred with > 99% frequency in all frames and the proportion of plots with > 25% cover ranged from 84- 100%. In general, there was an increase in cheatgrass cover from 2009 to 2012. The Pump Station frame had the highest overall cheatgrass cover with over 67% of plots having cheatgrass cover >75%. This expansion in cheatgrass cover is likely a product of the Long Butte fire and may have been exasperated by two higher than average months of precipitation in January and March 2012 (Appendix C). Tumble mustard, a Eurasian annual forb indicative of rangeland degradation, had a higher frequency and percent cover than any other nonnative invasive forb, occurring with >5% cover in 2%-22% of plots in HAFO, with the North and South frames having the highest rates of tumble mustard.

The combination of very low sagebrush cover, low native grass and forb cover, and high non-native invasive grass and forb cover in HAFO is very telling and these indicators show that the sagebrush steppe vegetation component within the monument is highly degraded, exacerbated by the 2010 Long Butte Fire. This dynamic, referred to as the "fire-cheatgrass cycle", is typical of many areas in the Snake River Plain. Big sagebrush cover was much lower than 2009 pre-fire levels and the comparison of cheat grass abundance from 2009 to 2012 (Table 3 and Appendix D) shows that the proportion of plots with cover values >25% for cheatgrass are 84-100% for the 5 frames and represent an increase for all frames. The recent disturbance caused by the Long Butte Fire and the loss of big sagebrush and native perennial grass and forb, as well as the increase in bareground cover, has left conditions very suitable for accelerated non-native grass and forb invasion.

Table 3. Summary statistics for estimated cheatgrass infestation in HAFO, 2009 and 2012.

North	2012	2009
Total acreage sampled	112.46	108.74
Total with no cheatgrass	0.00	0.00
Proportion of total frame area with no cheatgrass	0.00	0.00
Total with at least some cheatgrass	112.46	108.74
Proportion of total strata area with cheatgrass	1.00	1.00
Heavily infested acreage (>25% cover)	112.46	100.04
Proportion of heavily infested	1.00	0.92
Oregon Trail	2012	2009
Total acreage sampled	536.56	677.73
Total with no cheatgrass	0.00	45.18
Proportion of total frame area with no cheatgrass	0.00	0.07
Total with at least some cheatgrass	536.56	632.55
Proportion of total strata area with cheatgrass	1.00	0.93
Heavily infested acreage (>25% cover)	451.84	506.04
Proportion of heavily infested	0.84	0.75

Table 3 (continued). Summary statistics for estimated cheatgrass infestation in HAFO, 2009 and 2012.

Pump Station	2012	2009
Total acreage sampled	196.85	235.59
Total with no cheatgrass	7.16	4.28
Proportion of total frame area with no cheatgrass	0.04	0.02
Total with at least some cheatgrass	189.69	231.30
Proportion of total strata area with cheatgrass	0.96	0.98
Heavily infested acreage (>25% cover)	178.95	209.89
Proportion of heavily infested	0.91	0.89
South	**2012**	**2009**
Total acreage sampled	379.24	405.40
Total with no cheatgrass	0.00	18.71
Proportion of total frame area with no cheatgrass	0.00	0.05
Total with at least some cheatgrass	379.24	386.69
Proportion of total strata area with cheatgrass	1.00	0.95
Heavily infested acreage (>25% cover)	332.56	293.14
Proportion of heavily infested	0.88	0.72
Upper Bench	**2012**	**2009**
Total acreage sampled	83.18	130.68
Total with no cheatgrass	0.00	2.38
Proportion of total frame area with no cheatgrass	0.00	0.02
Total with at least some cheatgrass	83.18	128.31
Proportion of total strata area with cheatgrass	1.00	0.98
Heavily infested acreage (>25% cover)	69.57	92.67
Proportion of heavily infested	0.84	0.71

Literature Cited

Daubenmire, R.F. 1959. A canopy-coverage method. Northwest Science 33:43-64.

Erixson, J. A., and D. Cogan. 2009. Vegetation classification and mapping of Hagerman Fossil Beds National Monument. Natural Resource Technical Report NPS/UCBN/NRTR—2009/212. National Park Service, Fort Collins, Colorado.

Garrett, L. K., T. J. Rodhouse, G. H. Dicus, C. C. Caudill, and M. R. Shardlow. 2007. Upper Columbia Basin Network vital signs monitoring plan. Natural Resource Report NPS/UCBN/NRR-2007/002. National Park Service, Fort Collins, CO.

Rodhouse, T. J. 2010. Sagebrush steppe vegetation monitoring in Craters of the Moon National Monument and Preserve, Hagerman Fossil Beds National Monument, John Day Fossil Beds National Monument, and Lake Roosevelt National Recreation Area: 2009 annual report. Natural Resource Technical Report NPS/UCBN/NRTR—2010/302. National Park Service, Fort Collins, Colorado.

Stevens, D. L., and A. R. Olsen. 2004. Spatially balanced sampling of natural resources. Journal of the American Statistical Association 99:262-278.

Yeo, J. J., T. J. Rodhouse, G. H. Dicus, K. M. Irvine, and L. K. Garrett. 2009. Upper Columbia Basin Network sagebrush steppe vegetation monitoring protocol: Narrative version 1.0. Natural Resource Report NPS/UCBN/NRR—2009/142. National Park Service, Fort Collins, Colorado.

Appendix A: List of plant species mentioned in the report with common and scientific names.

Table A-1. Plant common, species, and updated species names.

Common name	Species name	Updated Species Name
Sagebrush		
Big sagebrush	*Artemisia tridentata*	
Other Shrubs		
Fourwing saltbush	*Atriplex canescens*	
Spiny saltbush	*Atriplex confertifolia*	
Green rabbitbrush	*Chrysothamnus viscidiflorus*	
Granite prickly phlox	*Leptodactylon pungens*	*Linanthus pungens*
Greasewood	*Sarcobatus vermiculatus*	
Native Grasses		
Western wheatgrass	*Agropyron smithii*	*Pascopyrum smithii*
Basin wildrye	*Elymus cinereus*	*Leymus cinereus*
Indian ricegrass	*Oryzopsis hymenoides*	*Achnatherum hymenoides*
Sandberg's, steppe bluegrass	*Poa secunda*	
Bluegrass spp	*Poa* spp	
Bluebunch wheatgrass	*Pseudoroegneria spicata*	
Squirreltail	*Sitanion hystrix*	*Elymus elymoides*
Needlegrass	*Stipa* spp	*Achnatherum*, <u>*Hesperostipa*</u>
Persistent Native Forbs		
Yarrow	*Achillea millefolium*	
Astragalus, Milkvetch	*Astragalus* spp	
Arrowleaf balsamroot	*Balsamorhiza sagittata*	
Indian paintbrush	*Castilleja* spp	
Dusty maiden	*Chaenactis douglasii*	
Native thistle	*Cirsium* spp	
Tapertip hawksbeard	*Crepis acuminata*	
Fleabane	*Erigeron* spp	
Biscuitroot	*Lomatium* spp	
Lupine	*Lupinus* spp	
Phlox	*Phlox* spp	
Ragwort	*Senecio* spp	
Desert princesplume	*Stanleya pinnata*	
Other Native Forbs		
Agoseris	*Agoseris* spp	
Onion	*Allium* spp	
Mariposa lily	*Calochortus* spp	
Larkspur	*Delphinium* spp	
Primrose	*Oenothera* spp	
Invasive Grasses		
Crested wheatgrass	*Agropyron cristatum*	
Cheatgrass	*Bromus tectorum*	
Bulbous bluegrass	*Poa bulbosa*	
Invasive Forbs		

Table A-1 (continued). Plant common, species, and updated species names.

Common name	Species name	Updated Species Name
Tansy mustard	*Descurainia* spp	
Filaree	*Erodium cicutarium*	
Clasping pepperweed	*Lepidium perfoliatum*	
Russian thistle	*Salsola kali*	
Tumble mustard	*Sisymbrium altissimum*	
Common salsify	*Tragopogon dubius*	

Appendix B. 2009 and 2012 sage monitoring data in HAFO: percentage of plots within each cover class for exposed bare ground and principal plant species organized by species guilds.

Table A-2. 2009 North sampling frame, HAFO: percentage of plots (n=50 1 m^2 plots) within each cover class for exposed bare ground and principal plant species organized by species guilds.

	0	1-5%	>5-25%	>25-50%	>50-75%	>75-95%	>95-100%
Bare Ground	56	36	6	0	0	2	0
Sagebrush							
Artemisia tridentata	56	6	12	8	10	8	0
Shrubs							
Atriplex canescens	98	2	0	0	0	0	0
Sarcobatus vermiculatus	98	0	0	0	0	2	0
Native Perennial Grasses							
Oryzopsis hymenoides	98	0	0	2	0	0	0
Poa secunda	70	18	12	0	0	0	0
Native Forbs (all)							
Forb spp	92	8	0	0	0	0	0
Non-native Invasive Forbs							
Descurainia sophia	66	12	20	2	0	0	0
Sisymbrium altissimum	94	2	4	0	0	0	0
Non-native Invasive Grasses							
Bromus tectorum	0	2	6	2	8	38	44

Table A-3. 2012 North sampling frame, HAFO: percentage of plots (n=50 1 m^2 plots) within each cover class for exposed bare ground and principal plant species organized by species guilds.

	0	1-5%	>5-25%	>25-50%	>50-75%	>75-95%	>95-100%
Bare ground	12	40	42	4	2	0	0
Sagebrush							
Artemisia tridentata	100	0	0	0	0	0	0
Shrubs							
Sarcobatus vermiculatus	94	0	2	4	0	0	0
Native Perennial Grasses							
Poa secunda	42	10	30	16	2	0	0
Native Persistent Forbs							
none	-	-	-	-	-	-	-
Native Other Forbs							
none	-	-	-	-	-	-	-
Non-native Invasive Forbs							
Descurainia spp	98	2	0	0	0	0	0
Erodium cicutarium	86	14	0	0	0	0	0
Lepidium perfoliatum	98	0	2	0	0	0	0
Salsola kali	98	0	2	0	0	0	0
Sisymbrium altissimum	52	26	16	4	2	0	0
Tragopogon dubius	98	2	0	0	0	0	0
Non-native Invasive Grasses							
Bromus tectorum	0	0	0	6	52	36	6

Table A-4. 2009 Oregon Trail sampling frame, HAFO: percentage of plots (n=75 1 m^2 plots) within each cover class for exposed bare ground and principal plant species organized by species guilds.

	0	1-5%	>5-25%	>25-50%	>50-75%	>75-95%	>95-100%
Bare Ground	57	29	12	1	0	0	0
Sagebrush							
Artemisia tridentata	81	1	9	4	1	3	0
Shrubs							
Atriplex canescens	95	0	4	0	0	1	0
Atriplex confertifolia	99	0	1	0	0	0	0
Chrysothamnus viscidiflorus	83	5	8	1	1	1	0
Eurotia lanata	99	0	1	0	0	0	0
Grayia spinosa	99	0	0	1	0	0	0
Purshia tridentata	99	0	0	0	0	1	0
Sarcobatus vermiculatus	99	1	0	0	0	0	0
Native Perennial Grasses							
Oryzopsis hymenoides	99	1	0	0	0	0	0
Poa secunda	39	33	16	9	3	0	0
Sitanion hystrix	91	4	5	0	0	0	0
Native Forbs (all)							
Forb spp	72	20	8	0	0	0	0
Non-native Invasive Forbs							
Descurainia sophia	81	17	1	0	0	0	0
Sisymbrium altissimum	67	17	11	4	1	0	0
Non-native Invasive Grasses							
Agropyron cristatum	76	4	12	4	3	1	0
Bromus tectorum	7	3	16	20	21	29	4
Poa bulbosa	99	0	0	0	1	0	0

Table A-5. 2012 Oregon Trail sampling frame, HAFO: percentage of plots (n=76 1 m^2 plots) within each cover class for exposed bare ground and principal plant species organized by species guilds.

	0	1-5%	>5-25%	>25-50%	>50-75%	>75-95%	>95-100%
Bare ground	26	42	20	9	3	0	0
Sagebrush							
Artemisia tridentata	99	1	0	0	0	0	0
Shrubs							
Atriplex canescens	97	1	1	0	0	0	0
Chrysothamnus viscidiflorus	92	7	1	0	0	0	0
Leptodactylon pungens	99	1	0	0	0	0	0
Sarcobatus vermiculatus	99	0	0	0	1	0	0
Native Perennial Grasses							
Agropyron smithii	95	0	3	0	3	0	0
Elymus cinereus	99	0	1	0	0	0	0
Oryzopsis hymenoides	97	1	1	0	0	0	0
Poa secunda	80	4	9	3	4	0	0
Sitanion hystrix	92	3	5	0	0	0	0
Stipa spp	99	0	1	0	0	0	0
Native Persistent Forbs							
Achillea millefolium	99	1	0	0	0	0	0
Astragalus spp	96	4	0	0	0	0	0
Balsamorhiza sagittata	97	3	0	0	0	0	0
Crepis acuminata	84	11	4	1	0	0	0
Phlox spp	92	5	3	0	0	0	0
Native Other Forbs							
Agoseris spp	97	3	0	0	0	0	0
Allium spp	91	9	0	0	0	0	0
Delphinium spp	99	1	0	0	0	0	0
Non-native Invasive Forbs							
Descurainia spp	96	3	1	0	0	0	0
Salsola kali	97	1	1	0	0	0	0
Sisymbrium altissimum	71	22	5	1	0	0	0
Tragopogon dubius	92	8	0	0	0	0	0
Non-native Invasive Grasses							
Agropyron cristatum	80	3	8	7	3	0	0
Bromus tectorum	0	3	13	11	14	32	28
Poa bulbosa	95	4	1	0	0	0	0

Table A-6. 2009 Pump Station sampling frame, HAFO: percentage of plots (n=55 1 m^2 plots) within each cover class for exposed bare ground and principal plant species organized by species guilds.

	0	1-5%	>5-25%	>25-50%	>50-75%	>75-95%	>95-100%
Bare Ground	53	35	5	7	0	0	0
Sagebrush							
Artemisia tridentata	56	5	16	5	7	9	0
Shrubs							
Atriplex canescens	93	4	0	0	2	0	2
Chrysothamnus nauseosus	96	2	2	0	0	0	0
Chrysothamnus viscidiflorus	95	2	2	2	0	0	0
Sarcobatus vermiculatus	89	2	0	7	2	0	0
Native Perennial Grasses							
Elymus cinereus	98	0	0	0	0	2	0
Oryzopsis hymenoides	98	0	2	0	0	0	0
Poa secunda	71	20	9	0	0	0	0
Sitanion hystrix	96	4	0	0	0	0	0
Native Forbs (all)							
Forb spp	93	4	4	0	0	0	0
Non-native Invasive Forbs							
Descurainia sophia	58	22	15	5	0	0	0
Sisymbrium altissimum	95	0	0	0	4	0	2
Non-native Invasive Grasses							
Bromus tectorum	2	2	7	7	20	53	9

Table A-7. 2012 Pump Station sampling frame, HAFO: percentage of plots (n=55 1 m2 plots) within each cover class for exposed bare ground and principal plant species organized by species guilds.

	0	1-5%	>5-25%	>25-50%	>50-75%	>75-95%	>95-100%
Bare ground	29	35	24	9	4	0	0
Sagebrush							
Artemisia tridentata	98	0	2	0	0	0	0
Shrubs							
Atriplex canescens	98	0	2	0	0	0	0
Atriplex confertifolia	98	2	0	0	0	0	0
Sarcobatus vermiculatus	76	11	4	5	2	2	0
Native Perennial Grasses							
Elymus cinereus	93	2	2	0	2	2	0
Poa secunda	71	11	13	2	4	0	0
Sitanion hystrix	98	0	2	0	0	0	0
Native Persistent Forbs							
Astragalus spp	98	0	2	0	0	0	0
Cirsium spp	98	2	0	0	0	0	0
Crepis acuminata	98	2	0	0	0	0	0
Lupinus spp	98	2	0	0	0	0	0
Stanleya pinnata	96	0	4	0	0	0	0
Native Other Forbs							
Allium spp	98	2	0	0	0	0	0
Non-native Invasive Forbs							
Descurainia spp	96	4	0	0	0	0	0
Lepidium perfoliatum	96	0	2	0	2	0	0
Salsola kali	98	2	0	0	0	0	0
Sisymbrium altissimum	76	15	5	4	0	0	0
Non-native Invasive Grasses							
Agropyron cristatum	96	0	2	0	2	0	0
Bromus tectorum	4	2	4	4	20	44	24

13

Table A-8. 2009 South sampling frame, HAFO: percentage of plots (n=65 1 m^2 plots) within each cover class for exposed bare ground and principal plant species organized by species guilds.

	0	1-5%	>5-25%	>25-50%	>50-75%	>75-95%	>95-100%
Bare Ground	42	40	12	5	0	2	0
Sagebrush							
Artemisia tridentata	69	5	12	8	2	5	0
Shrubs							
Artemisia spinescens	97	2	2	0	0	0	0
Atriplex canescens	88	3	5	3	2	0	0
Atriplex confertifolia	95	2	2	2	0	0	0
Chrysothamnus nauseosus	97	0	0	3	0	0	0
Chrysothamnus viscidiflorus	75	6	8	8	3	0	0
Eurotia lanata	97	0	3	0	0	0	0
Sarcobatus vermiculatus	97	0	2	2	0	0	0
Native Perennial Grasses							
Elymus cinereus	98	0	2	0	0	0	0
Oryzopsis hymenoides	92	5	3	0	0	0	0
Poa secunda	43	31	15	8	3	0	0
Sitanion hystrix	83	11	5	2	0	0	0
Stipa spp	98	0	2	0	0	0	0
Native Forbs (all)							
Forb spp	58	28	11	3	0	0	0
Non-native Invasive Forbs							
Descurainia sophia	82	18	0	0	0	0	0
Sisymbrium altissimum	74	9	15	2	0	0	0
Non-native Invasive Grasses							
Agropyron cristatum	98	0	2	0	0	0	0
Bromus tectorum	5	6	17	17	22	29	5

Table A-9. 2012 South sampling frame, HAFO: percentage of plots (n=65 1 m^2 plots) within each cover class for exposed bare ground and principal plant species organized by species guilds.

	0	1-5%	>5-25%	>25-50%	>50-75%	>75-95%	>95-100%
Bare ground	31	46	18	3	0	0	2
Sagebrush							
Artemisia tridentata	98	2	0	0	0	0	0
Shrubs							
Atriplex canescens	98	0	0	2	0	0	0
Atriplex confertifolia	97	3	0	0	0	0	0
Chrysothamnus viscidiflorus	91	5	5	0	0	0	0
Leptodactylon pungens	94	3	3	0	0	0	0
Sarcobatus vermiculatus	97	2	0	2	0	0	0
Native Perennial Grasses							
Elymus cinereus	98	0	0	2	0	0	0
Oryzopsis hymenoides	94	2	3	0	2	0	0
Poa secunda	68	18	9	3	2	0	0
Poa spp	98	0	0	0	2	0	0
Sitanion hystrix	88	8	5	0	0	0	0
Native Persistent Forbs							
Astragalus spp	97	2	2	0	0	0	0
Castilleja spp	98	2	0	0	0	0	0
Chaenactis douglasii	98	2	0	0	0	0	0
Crepis acuminata	97	3	0	0	0	0	0
Erigeron spp	98	2	0	0	0	0	0
Phlox spp	89	8	3	0	0	0	0
Senecio spp	98	2	0	0	0	0	0
Stanleya pinnata	98	2	0	0	0	0	0
Native Other Forbs							
Allium spp	97	3	0	0	0	0	0
Calochortus spp	97	3	0	0	0	0	0
Delphinium spp	98	2	0	0	0	0	0
Oenothera spp	98	2	0	0	0	0	0
Non-native Invasive Forbs							
Descurainia spp	80	12	3	2	3	0	0
Sisymbrium altissimum	66	18	12	3	0	0	0
Tragopogon dubius	94	6	0	0	0	0	0
Non-native Invasive Grasses							
Agropyron cristatum	98	0	0	2	0	0	0
Bromus tectorum	0	5	8	11	17	29	31

Table A-10. 2009 Upper Bench sampling frame, HAFO: percentage of plots (n=55 1 m^2 plots) within each cover class for exposed bare ground and principal plant species organized by species guilds.

	0	1-5%	>5-25%	>25-50%	>50-75%	>75-95%	>95-100%
Bare Ground	35	49	5	4	2	5	0
Sagebrush							
Artemisia tridentata	75	5	7	9	4	0	0
Shrubs							
Chrysothamnus nauseosus	87	4	4	4	2	0	0
Chrysothamnus viscidiflorus	67	15	11	7	0	0	0
Purshia tridentata	98	2	0	0	0	0	0
Sarcobatus vermiculatus	98	2	0	0	0	0	0
Native Perennial Grasses							
Elymus cinereus	95	5	0	0	0	0	0
Oryzopsis hymenoides	96	4	0	0	0	0	0
Poa secunda	29	31	15	13	11	2	0
Sitanion hystrix	89	9	2	0	0	0	0
Stipa spp	98	0	2	0	0	0	0
Native Forbs (all)							
Forb spp	64	31	5	0	0	0	0
Non-native Invasive Forbs							
Descurainia sophia	71	27	2	0	0	0	0
Sisymbrium altissimum	84	9	5	2	0	0	0
Non-native Invasive Grasses							
Agropyron cristatum	85	2	5	7	0	0	0
Bromus tectorum	2	7	20	25	22	18	5

Table A-11. 2012 Upper Bench sampling frame, HAFO: percentage of plots (n=55 1 m^2 plots) within each cover class for exposed bare ground and principal plant species organized by species guilds.

	0	1-5%	>5-25%	>25-50%	>50-75%	>75-95%	>95-100%
Bare ground	9	45	38	2	2	4	0
Sagebrush							
Artemisia tridentata	100	0	0	0	0	0	0
Shrubs							
Atriplex canescens	98	0	2	0	0	0	0
Chrysothamnus viscidiflorus	96	4	0	0	0	0	0
Leptodactylon pungens	98	2	0	0	0	0	0
Native Perennial Grasses							
Agropyron smithii	84	4	2	9	2	0	0
Oryzopsis hymenoides	96	2	2	0	0	0	0
Poa secunda	62	4	11	11	13	0	0
Sitanion hystrix	87	4	5	4	0	0	0
Stipa spp	96	0	0	4	0	0	0
Native Persistent Forbs							
Achillea millefolium	96	4	0	0	0	0	0
Astragalus spp	98	2	0	0	0	0	0
Crepis acuminata	91	9	0	0	0	0	0
Erigeron spp	98	2	0	0	0	0	0
Lomatium spp	96	4	0	0	0	0	0
Lupinus spp	98	0	2	0	0	0	0
Phlox spp	87	9	4	0	0	0	0
Stanleya pinnata	95	2	4	0	0	0	0
Native Other Forbs							
Agoseris spp	98	2	0	0	0	0	0
Non-native Invasive Forbs							
Descurainia spp	98	2	0	0	0	0	0
Erodium cicutarium	98	2	0	0	0	0	0
Sisymbrium altissimum	93	5	2	0	0	0	0
Tragopogon dubius	95	5	0	0	0	0	0
Non-native Invasive Grasses							
Agropyron cristatum	84	2	15	0	0	0	0
Bromus tectorum	0	4	13	15	27	31	11

Appendix C: Climate diagrams for the Hagerman 2 SW weather station, near Hagerman Fossil Beds National Monument.

Figure A-1. This figure compares the long-term (30 yrs) averages of monthly temperatures (red line) and monthly precipitation (blue line). The period when the temperature line exceeds the precipitation line defines the arid period for plant growth. Individual monthly data was not included in figures if more than 5 days of data was lacking.

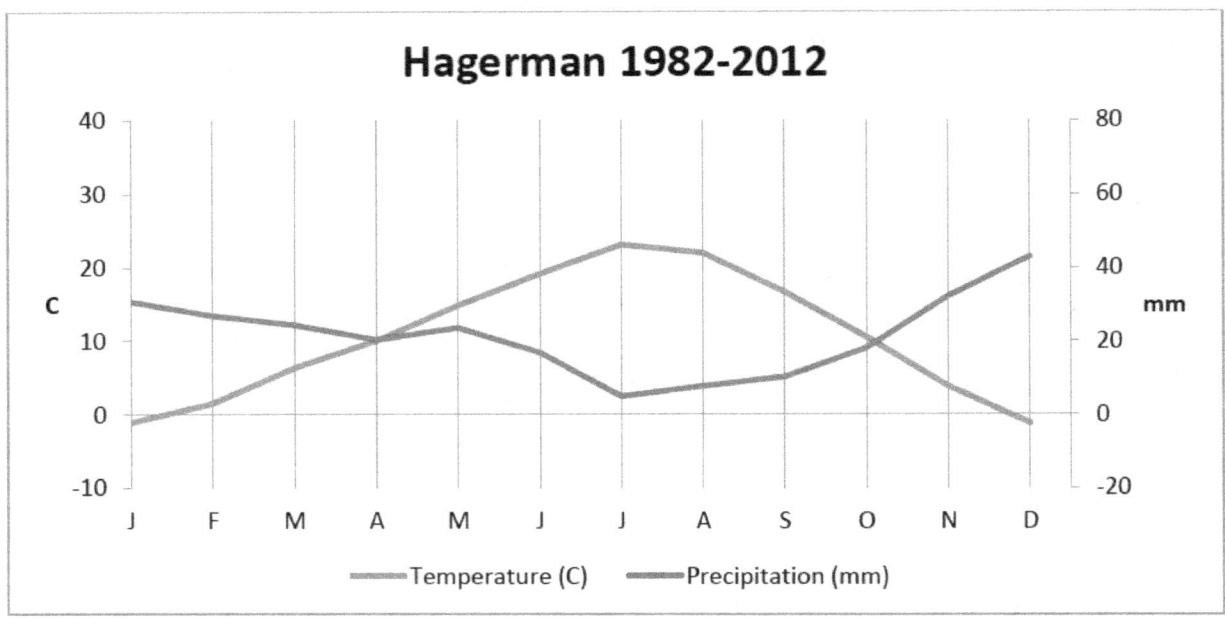

Figure A-2. This figure compares the averages of monthly temperatures (red line) and monthly precipitation (blue line) in 2009. The period when the temperature line exceeds the precipitation line defines the arid period for plant growth. Individual monthly data was not included in figures if more than 5 days of data was lacking.

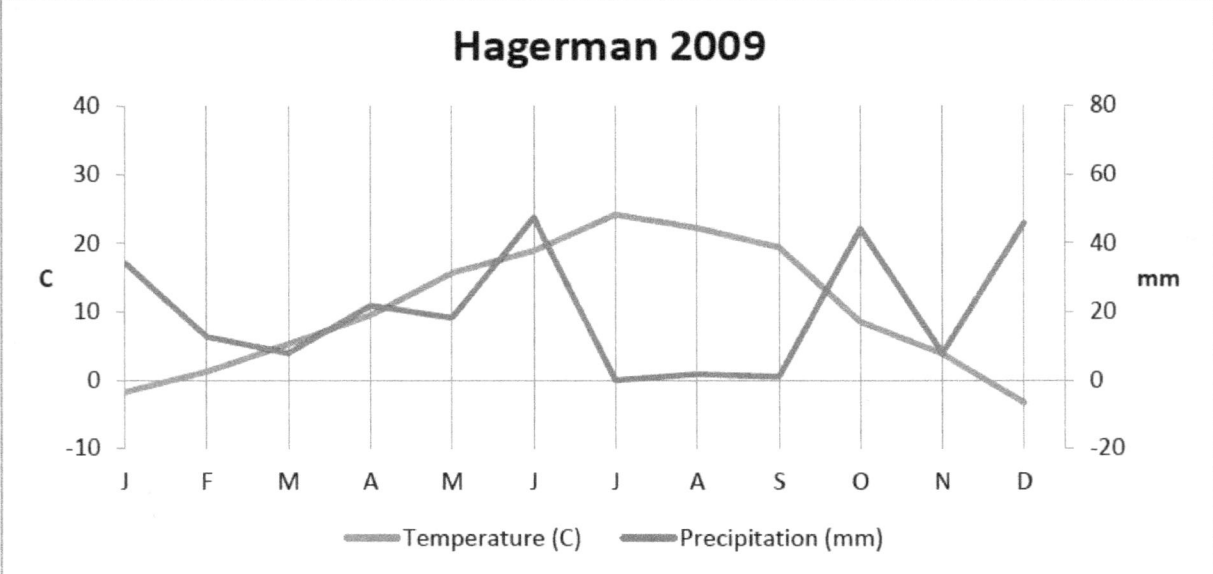

18

Figure A-3. This figure compares the averages of monthly temperatures (red line) and monthly precipitation (blue line) in 2010. The period when the temperature line exceeds the precipitation line defines the arid period for plant growth. Individual monthly data was not included in figures if more than 5 days of data was lacking.

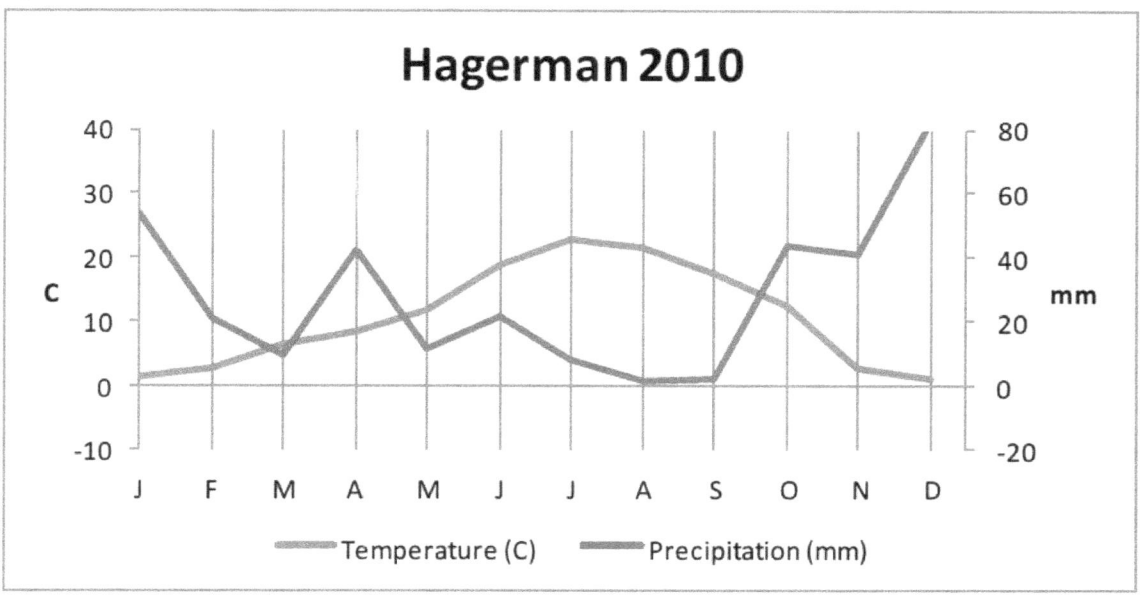

Figure A-4. This figure compares the averages of monthly temperatures (red line) and monthly precipitation (blue line) in 2011. The period when the temperature line exceeds the precipitation line defines the arid period for plant growth. Individual monthly data was not included in figures if more than 5 days of data was lacking.

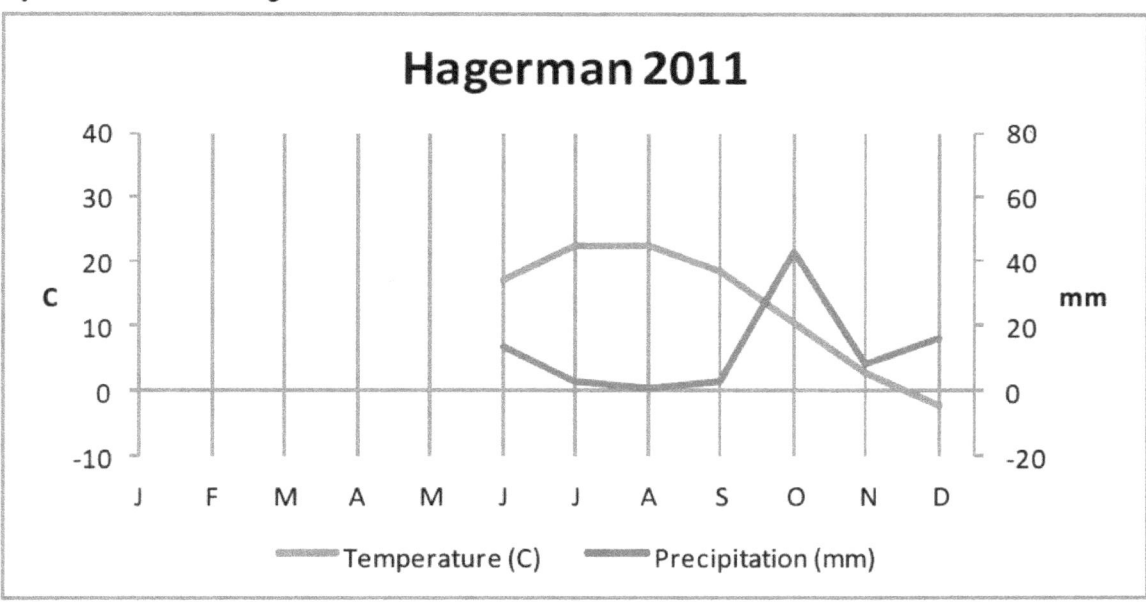

Figure A-5. This figure compares the averages of monthly temperatures (red line) and monthly precipitation (blue line) in 2012. The period when the temperature line exceeds the precipitation line defines the arid period for plant growth. Individual monthly data was not included in figures if more than 5 days of data was lacking.

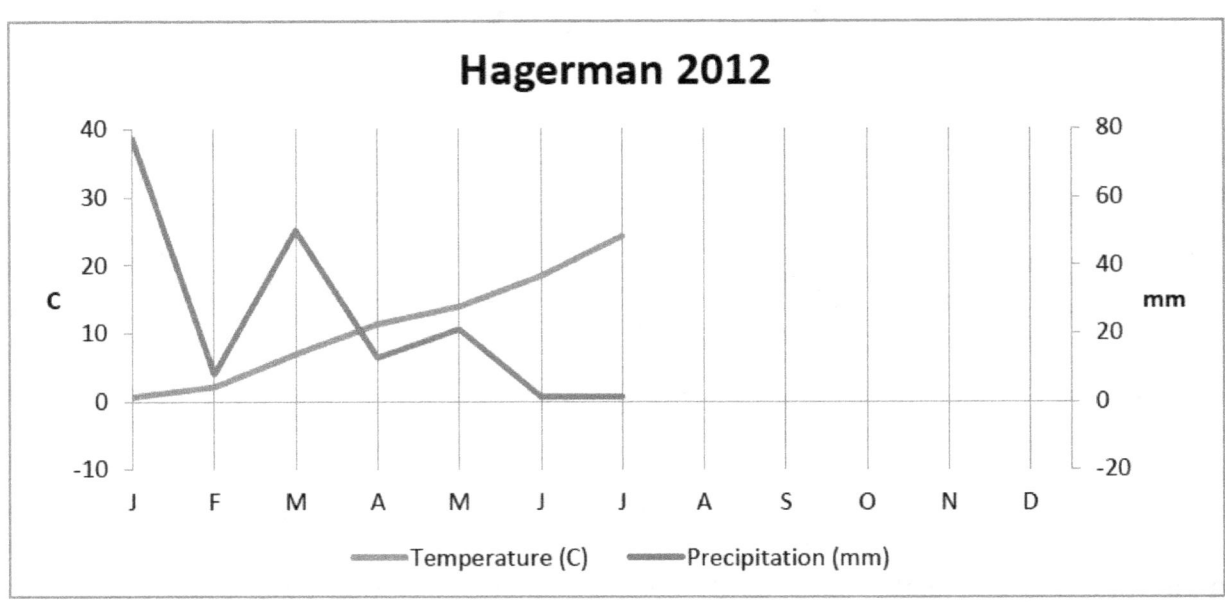

Appendix D. Bar graphs comparing 2009 and 2012 cheatgrass cover estimates in Hagerman Fossil Beds National Monument

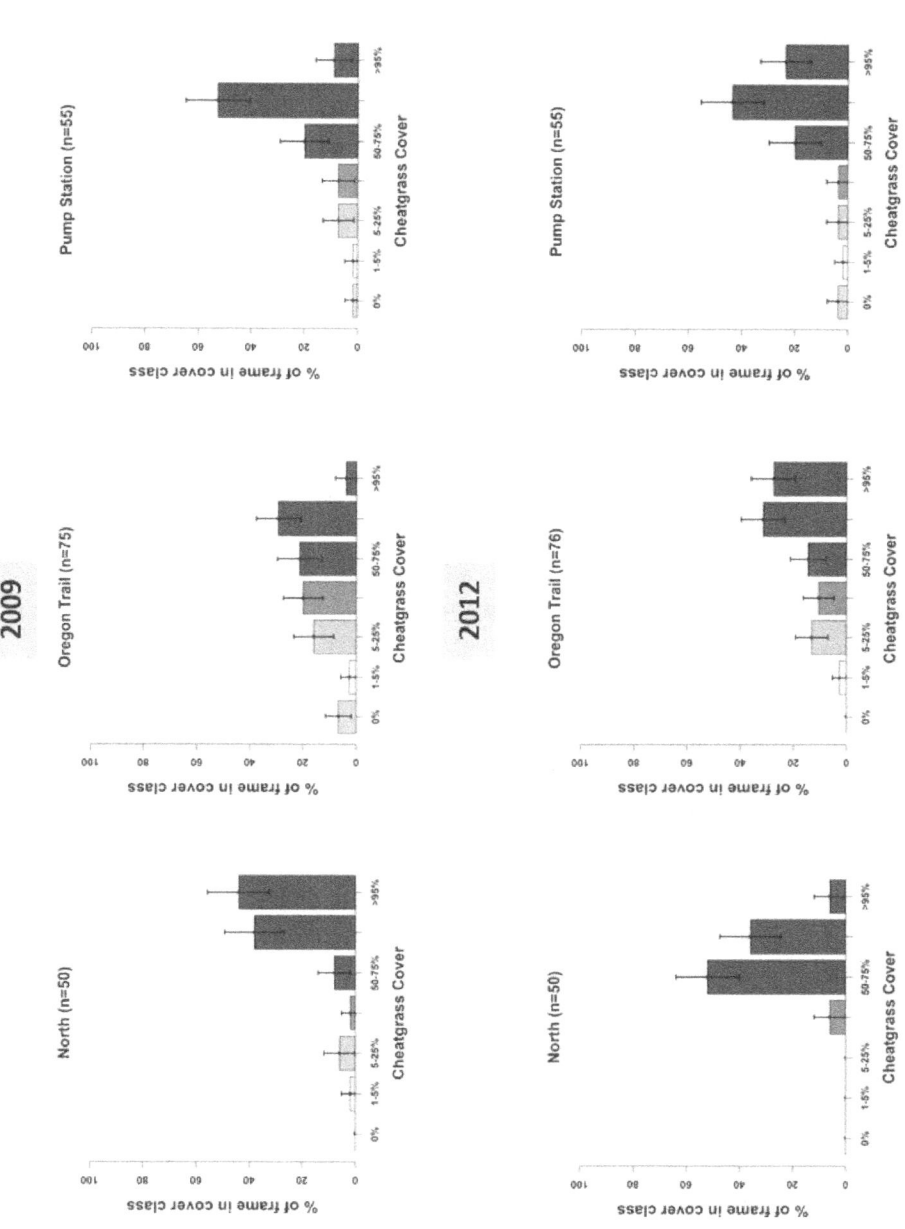

Figure A-6. Estimated frame area (from proportion of plots) and 95% confidence intervals (estimated with the local "grts" efficient variance estimator; Stevens and Olsen [2004]) in each cover class for cheatgrass in (top) 2009 and (bottom) 2012.

Figure A-6 (continued). Estimated strata area (from proportion of plots) and 95% confidence intervals (estimated with the local "grts" efficient variance estimator; Stevens and Olsen [2004]) in each cover class for cheatgrass in (top) 2011 and (bottom) 2012.

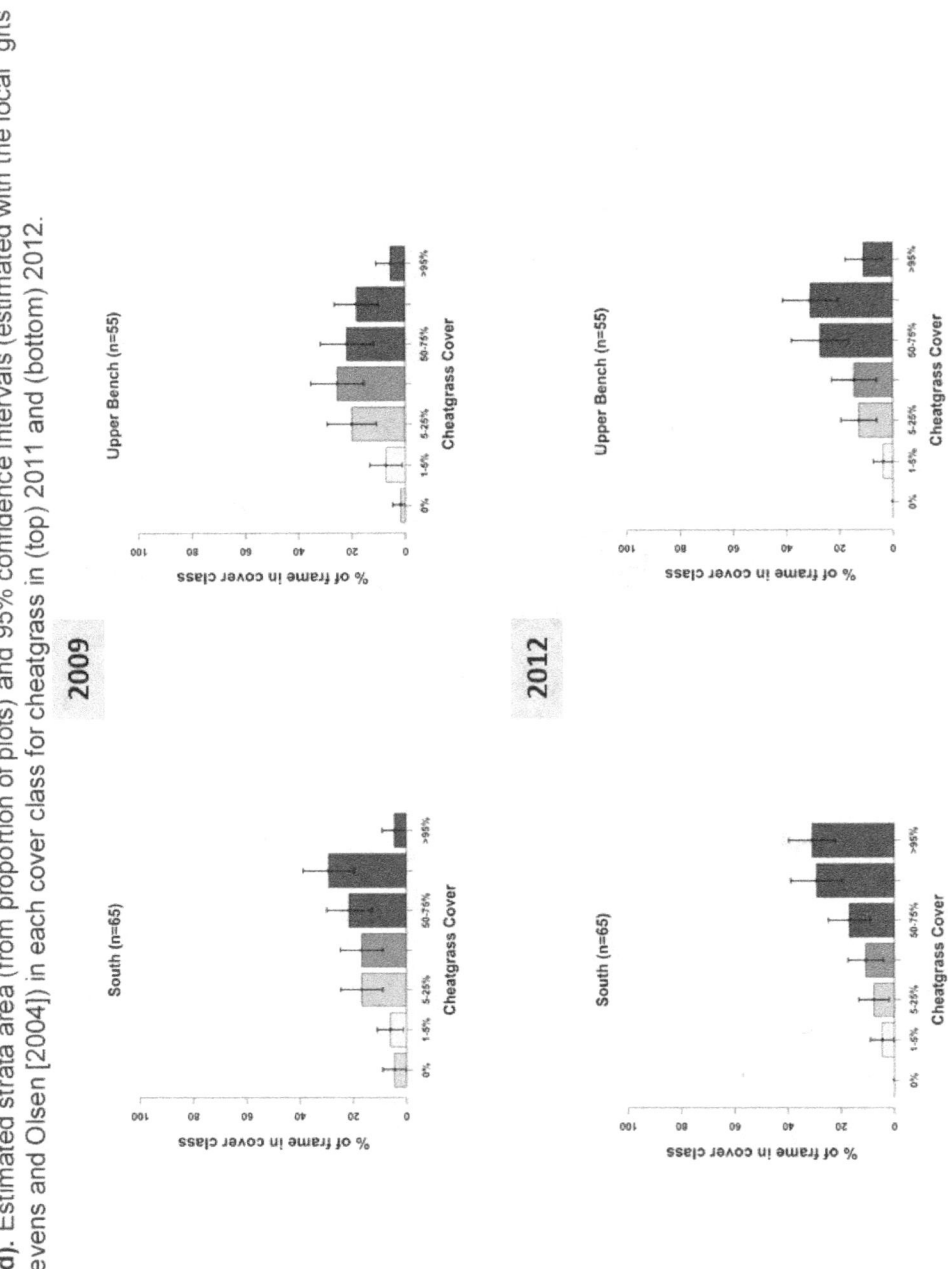